PRESENTS

You Know You're Dutch, When...

Words by Colleen Geske

Production by kchiing publishing

Published in the Netherlands
by Stuff Dutch People Like

Some of the material in this book may have originally
appeared, in different form, on the popular blog
StuffDutchPeopleLike.com

Photo & other credits can be found on page 206

ISBN 978-90-821336-5-3

Printed in the EU

10 9 8 7 6 5 4 3 2 1

www.stuffdutchpeoplelike.com
www.facebook.com/stuffdutchpeoplelike
www.instagram.com/stuffdutchpeoplelike
www.twitter.com/stuffdutchlike

For media inquiries, corporate & volume sales
or any other requests, please contact us at
hello@stuffdutchpeoplelike.com

YOU KNOW YOU'RE DUTCH WHEN...

by Colleen Geske

People always ask if I have anything left to say about Dutch people. The answer is simple: why, of course I do! I'll even make you a promise: if you Dutch people keep up your weird and wonderful wacky ways, I'll keep writing about them for the whole wide world to know, love and appreciate.

Consider this book yet another love-letter dedicated to all the Dutchies (and Dutch wannabees) scattered across the globe. I've had one heck of a good time putting together the ultimate list of what really makes a Dutch person Dutch. I hope it gives you a few belly laughs along the way. Never stop being you. Deal? Deal!

xo,
Colleen

You're an adult & still love chocolate sprinkles on bread.

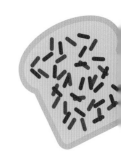

Hagelslag was first brought to the market by the Dutch company Venz in 1936. Legend has it that the company's owner was inspired by a letter from a 5-year-old boy, requesting a chocolate bread topping! #smartkid

DID YOU KNOW?

The Dutch eat over 14 million kilos of *hagelslag* each year. That's 750,000 slices of bread topped with *hagelslag* every day! Yum!

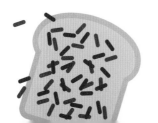

7

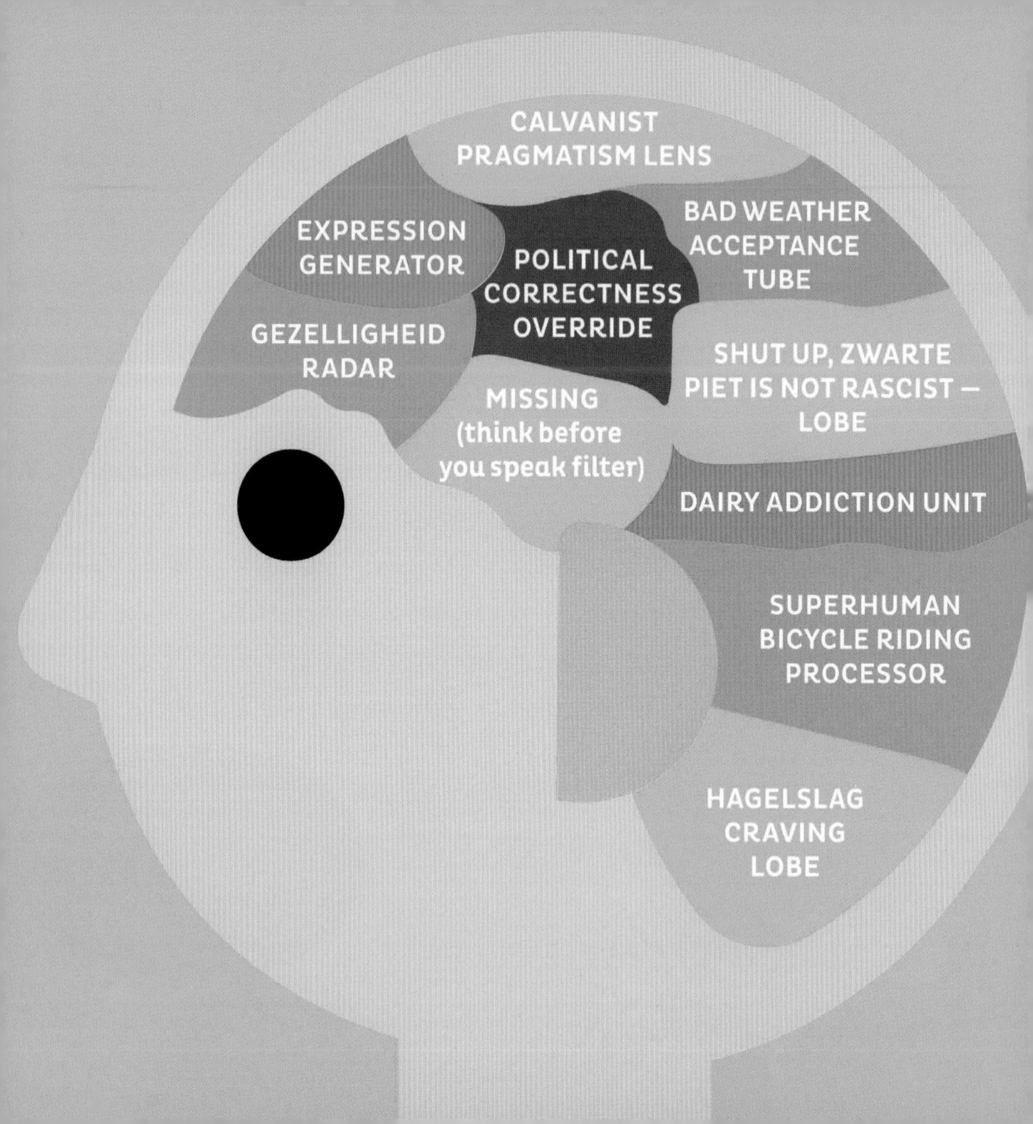
CALVANIST PRAGMATISM LENS
EXPRESSION GENERATOR
POLITICAL CORRECTNESS OVERRIDE
BAD WEATHER ACCEPTANCE TUBE
GEZELLIGHEID RADAR
SHUT UP, ZWARTE PIET IS NOT RASCIST — LOBE
MISSING (think before you speak filter)
DAIRY ADDICTION UNIT
SUPERHUMAN BICYCLE RIDING PROCESSOR
HAGELSLAG CRAVING LOBE

This is pretty much what your brain looks like.

You think bicycle helmets are ridiculous.

The Netherlands have fewer head injuries caused by bicycle accidents than other nations —even with an almost complete lack of protective headgear. The Dutch are taught how and when to watch for bicyclists from the first time they sit behind the wheel of a car. The vast majority of Dutch bike paths are safely separated from vehicular traffic, which results in fewer bike-to-car interactions and fewer collisions.

11

Your favourite holiday destination is a campground.

In the summer of 2017 some 550,000 Dutch caravans and campers were expected to hit the roads — an all-time high! Sales of campers in May of 2017 rose by 59% compared to the year prior. It looks like Dutchies and their love of camping are here to stay!

DID YOU KNOW?

Google Trends ranks the Netherlands as the TOP nation for Internet searches for the word 'camping' *(kamperen)*, followed by France and Denmark. Numbers don't lie!

You chant "Hup Holland Hup" at a football match, but lecture foreigners that your country is called "The Netherlands".

The official name of the Lowlands is actually the Kingdom of the Netherlands. The term 'Holland' only represents the two Dutch provinces of Noord-Holland and South-Holland. The national tourists board, along with KLM and the Holland-American Cruise Line, can be blamed for much of the confusion, as they have been extensively marketing the country abroad as 'Holland' since the early 1950s.

You'll take any excuse to meet in a bar, have a beer and eat fried snacks. Borreltijd!

The term *Vrijmibo* is the short-form for after-work drinks on a Friday. (Vrij=*Vrijdag*, Mi=*Middag*, Bo=*Borrel*).

So what exactly is a *borrel*?
1. An informal designation for a small glass of spirits.
2. A social gathering of a select (invited) group, often with a theme or occasion.
3. Having a damn good time with your co-workers!

You have interesting new year's traditions.

You eat dinner at 6pm sharp. Doesn't everyone?

Wander the Dutch streets at 6pm in any given town and you may wonder whether the zombie apocalypse has begun. *Where are all the people? The children? The cats? The dogs? Should I run and hide?* Nah, you just need to get better at following the rules and chow down at the socially-acceptable prescribed time. *Eet smakelijk!*

21

You can pronounce "Scheveningen" without hurting yourself.

It is said that the name of the tricky-to-pronounce Dutch seaside town of Scheveningen was used as a *shibboleth* during World War II to identify German spies. If a person could not properly pronounce the town, they were not to be trusted!

23

You hate having to pay 20 cents to use a public toilet.

In most Dutch shopping centers, department stores, gas stations, cafes, and bars, there is a price to be paid for using the porcelain throne. Pay your dues to the *toiletjuffrouw* (aka: the little old lady who doubles as the toilet bouncer) and you're in! If you're lucky, she may just let you have one of her urine-encrusted unwrapped mints. Bargain!

25

You congratulate everyone — & their brother — at a birthday party.

A mini-integration test of sorts, the Dutch birthday party is sure to confuse many an outsider. Because the Dutch appreciate a little *schadenfreude* (who doesn't?), they've made the well-wishes as complicated as possible for foreigners to pronounce. *Gefeliciteerd* will take some practice to master, but a muffled mouthful of throaty G's —said with confidence—will do just fine in a pinch.

You eagerly tell foreigners that Santa Claus is based on Sinterklaas.

Closely-related Sinterklaas figures actually exist in Germany, Switzerland, Austria, Belgium, and French Flanders. Even the Scandinavians have some 'Nisse' guy who looks an awful lot like Santa. The Dutch like to stake claim for starting the 'old bearded white guy with presents' trend, but he seems to pop up a lot in European history books. Just saying.

Can someone explain why Santa gained a good 40 kilos when crossing the Atlantic ocean? We're guessing it was a hearty overseas supply of *stroopwafels* and *pepernoten*...

You'd like Germans to stop digging holes on Dutch beaches.

Your agenda is fully booked for the next 4 months.

The Dutch are many things but 'spontaneous' is not one of them. Highly efficient planners, the Dutch-agenda (or modern day smartphone) takes center stage in almost all Dutch workand personal relationships. Play the game, or lose out!

33

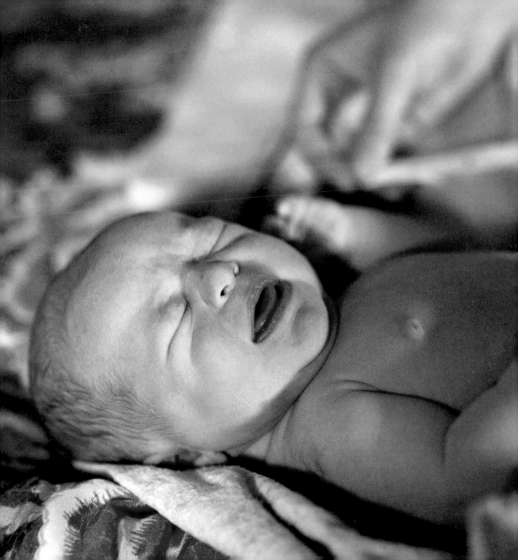

Someone in your family was born at home.

The Dutch are pioneers of the home birth. Although numbers have decreased over time a whopping 14% of all births in the Netherlands take place at home. A large-scale study (of some 147,000 low-risk births) released in 2013 concluded that low-risk home births in the Netherlands were in fact safer than hospital births.

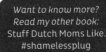

Want to know more? Read my other book: Stuff Dutch Moms Like. #shamelessplug

35

You love to remind Americans that New York was once Dutch.

In 1625, Dutch settlers founded 'Nieuw-Amsterdam' (New Amsterdam) as the capital of 'Nieuw-Nederland' (New Netherlands) on the southern tip of Manhattan. Some twenty years later, New Amsterdam was conquered by the English and re-named after the Duke of York. #historylesson

DID YOU KNOW?

Brooklyn, Broadway, Harlem, Wall Street, Long Island, and the Bronx all derive their names from Dutch words or towns.

37

You love feeding dubbelzoute drop to foreigners.

Dutch licorice tastes like soiled socks mixed with cleaning products and a dash of salt. An acquired taste, it's nothing like its English or American counterparts.

"When I was a kid I thought it was just us that did this. Turns out Dutch people all over the world have the same humor." – from our blog comments

You own several pieces of orange clothing.

In the Netherlands, *Oranje* can refer to many things: the Royal family, the national football team, or the colour itself! When in doubt, just throw on some orange gear and head to the streets!

You love practical solutions to everyday problems.

The Dutch are known the world over for their pragmatic approach to sex (legalized prostitution), drugs (decriminalized marijuana), and even death (liberal euthanasia practices). They are keen to find innovative solutions to common problems.

DID YOU KNOW?

Dutch criminals, if found to have been conducting financially lucrative illegal businesses, must pay "back-taxes" on their gains.

43

You always ask for a receipt & double-check if everything is correct.

The Dutch have a long-standing tradition of being 'thrifty' and rather careful with their cash, but paradoxically the Netherlands is also known as one of the most generous countries when it comes to charity and individual donations (second only to those rich bastards in Luxembourg, Sweden, and Norway).

You wash your hands with ice cold water in a tiny sink after using the toilet.

We ain't gonna lie, after living in the Netherlands for over a decade, we still haven't adapted to the glacial H2O that flows from the taps of those teeny-tiny sinks. The simple act of washing your hands without gasping from the arctic temperatures would go a long way on a cold Dutch winter's day.

"It's cold because it's meant for washing your hands, not taking a relaxing shower, you wally!" – Blog commenter, Peter D. (who is clearly Dutch and rather direct).

47

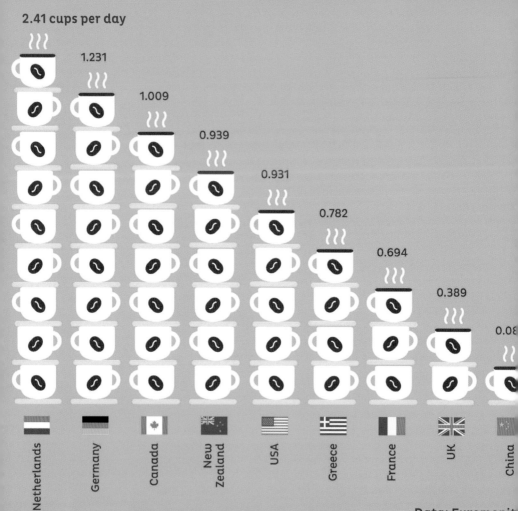

2.41 cups per day

1.231

1.009

0.939

0.931

0.782

0.694

0.389

0.08

Netherlands
Germany
Canada
New Zealand
USA
Greece
France
UK
China

Data: Euromonit

You drink more than two cups of coffee per day.

The Dutch are the largest consumers of coffee in the world. When visiting the Netherlands for the first time, don't go confusing all those 'coffee shops' for, well, coffee shops. You will find mind-altering, addictive substances in both, some more potent than others.

49

You know the difference between pepernoten & kruidnoten.

... or rather, you know the difference between *pepernoten* and *kruidnoten* and yet still refuse to call the hard round ones (as pictured) by their correct name: *kruidnoten!!*

You swear with ancient diseases.

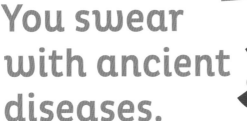

If you're going to spend time in the Netherlands, you had better brush up on your knowledge of rare diseases from years gone by. The more serious your offense, the more serious the disease in question. Typhoid, tuberculosis, cholera, small pox, the plague, and more recently, the Big C (*kanker*), can all rear their ugly heads. 'Swearing-by-disease' is in fact a unique Dutch trait—no other language or culture in the world has similar curses.

DID YOU KNOW?

A survey by the Dutch *Bond Tegen Vloeken* (aka: the Federation against Swearing. *Yup, this exists.*) deemed that *kanker* (cancer) was the most 'hurtful' of swear words. Don't say it, folks: #karma.

You buy your deep-fried snacks out of a wall.

The name FEBO comes from the street in Amsterdam where the first fast-food store was located: Ferdinand Bolstraat. Founded in 1941, FEBO is known for its signature automatic snack vending-machines that stock piping-hot *kroketten*, *frikandellen*, *hamburgers*, *kaassoufflés*, and so on. FEBO has over 60 shops in the Netherlands.

It drives you nuts when tourists only visit Amsterdam.

Many a tourist thinks Amsterdam is the only place worthy of a visit in the Netherlands, but of course, we know that is simply not the case. Venture outside *Mokum* and you will encounter unspoiled beauty and adventure. My favourite spot? Don't ask me, I've never left Amsterdam. #whywouldi? #jokingnotjoking

De zuigers zijn buiten werking.

De directie

The suckers are out working.

The direction

You're fluent in Dunglish.

When asked what he does as a hobby, a Dutch man proudly replies: "I fok horses". (*Fok=breed*). Shocked, the English-speaking man exclaims: "Pardon?!?" The Dutch man smiles, and nods, "Yes, Paarden!!" (*Paarden=horses*)

** A long-standing urban legend claims that this conversation actually took place between JFK and Dutch politician Joseph Luns.

This is your favourite lunch.

You own more than one bike.

...and you've had it stolen at least once.

DID YOU KNOW?

Amsterdam has some 810,000 people and more than 1 million bicycles. The worst places for bike theft are Groningen, Vlieland, Nijmegen, and Maastricht, so we're guessing their bike-to-people ratio is a little less ...

You eagerly await eating a chocolate letter of your first initial every year.

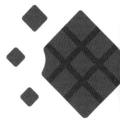

◆ Chocolate letters come in all sizes and fonts.

◆ In the 16th and 17th centuries, pastry letters, not chocolate, were given as presents.

◆ Chocolate letters first appeared in the 20th century, and were an immediate hit.

◆ Q, U, X, Y or Z are pretty difficult to find, as most manufacturers don't even make them.

◆ Albert Heijn—that famous Dutch supermarket—guarantees to stock all letters, which is great news for little Quint and his brother Zander.

◆ Canadians import over 1 million Dutch chocolate letters each year (what a greedy bunch!).

You can leave the Netherlands, but it never leaves you.

According to Wikipedia, there are more than 15 million people of Dutch heritage living abroad! Here's a quick overview:

Dutch Americans 5 million

Afrikaners 2.7 million

Dutch Canadians 1 million

Dutch Australians 340,000

Dutch New Zealanders 100,000

67

You have a friend whose name sounds hilarious in English.

The Dutch have a term for these unfortunate names: *schaamnaam* (which directly translates to 'shame-name'). The Dutch radio station 3FM runs a yearly contest for the most shameful name in the nation. No surprise, Fokje Modder is the 'all-time winner'!

You have no credit card debt.

Some would say that debt is as American as apple pie. The Dutch make a mean *appeltaart,* but their American counterparts still run circles around them when it comes to racking up credit card debt. In 2016, the average US household had a whopping $17,000 of credit card debt. The Dutch rarely use credit cards at home (only about 3% of all non-cash transactions) and have hardly any credit card debt.

You believe it's your duty to tell your friend that her new haircut doesn't suit her.

You'll cycle through a storm to avoid taking a taxi.

Most Dutch don't shy away from a little rain, or a lot of rain, for that matter. According to the *Fietsersbond* (the Dutch cyclists' union) 82% of Dutchies will brave the weather and cycle in 'strong rain.'

You've told visitors it's dinnertime, meaning time for them to leave.

Although you can buy marijuana whenever you want, you don't use it.

According to the World Drug Report, below are the figures for annual prevalence usage of cannabis (i.e. 15-64 year olds who have consumed cannabis at least once in the past year):

Iceland: 18.3%
United States: 16.2%
Canada: 12.7%
France: 11%
Australia: 10.6%
Spain: 9.2%
Netherlands: 8%

VERJAARDAGSKALENDER

1 Harm
2
3
4
5
6 Freek
7

8
9
10
11 Joke
12
13
14

15
16
17 Sicco
18
19
20
21
22 Taco

23
24
25
26
27
28 Door
29
30
31

January

You have a birthday calendar in your toilet.

. . . well, not exactly in your toilet. Like, not sitting at the bottom of your toilet getting all wet and stinky. But I was trying to use your local lingo, folks. In Canada we say "washroom" or "bathroom," but you Dutchies get straight to the point. One needn't ask where the bathroom is, when you can simply say "*Toilet?*".

81

ENGLISH PROFICIENCY RANKING (2016)

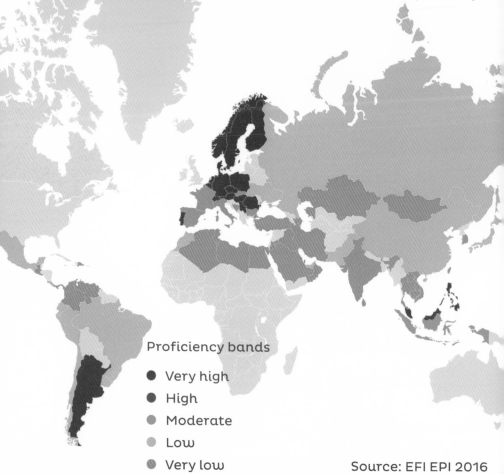

Proficiency bands

- Very high
- High
- Moderate
- Low
- Very low

Source: EFI EPI 2016

You speak English better than some Canadians.

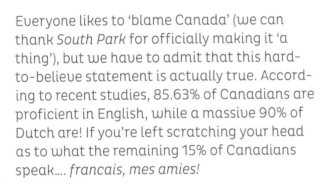

Everyone likes to 'blame Canada' (we can thank *South Park* for officially making it 'a thing'), but we have to admit that this hard-to-believe statement is actually true. According to recent studies, 85.63% of Canadians are proficient in English, while a massive 90% of Dutch are! If you're left scratching your head as to what the remaining 15% of Canadians speak.... *francais, mes amies!*

Semper Augu...

Your ancestors once paid 10x their yearly salary for a tulip bulb.

Although incomprehensible, at their height of Golden-Age-popularity, a single tulip bulb could fetch 10 times the annual salary of a skilled Dutch worker or as much as a gorgeous picturesque canal house. In 1637, however, irrational enthusiasm for the flowers triggered a speculative frenzy and the tulip market took a dive like no other. Many a Dutchie lost their entire fortune in what came to be known as *tulipmania*.

You split the bill on your first date. And maybe your second.

'Going Dutch': a common expression, meaning to pay for one's own food or to split the bill at a restaurant, is known the world over. Are the Dutch just downright cheap, or do they simply value equality? We'll let you ponder that one...

You go to Ikea for the cuisine.

You think you're invincible on a bicycle.

The Dutch believe there is some sort of invincibility cloak surrounding them while riding a bicycle. *Red lights?* What are those for?! *Traffic signs?* Those don't apply to me! *Cars?* Those suckers will just need to move out of the way! *Pedestrians?* Five points for making them scream. And 10 points for a near-collision! Let the games begin!!!!

91

You bring your own food & toilet paper on vacation with you.

- Toilet paper: 50.8%
- Coffee and/or tea: 40.6%
- Food: 30.9%
- Other drinks: 27.2%

Source: Hart van Nederland

You like to vote for a new government every 2 years.

The Dutch *poldermodel* seemed to provide relative stability; however, in recent years those *polders* seem to have sprung a leak. The system has been seriously shaken up by scandals, upheavals, politically-motivated murders, as well as general fear-mongering and anti-immigrant sentiment. Will the next 10 years be as juicy? We're kinda hoping not.

You don't expect to get any gifts for Valentine's day (but secretly wish you did!).

You think Nasi Goreng is a Dutch dish.

You love mashing your food.

We've said it before and we will say it again, Dutch people have 3 very specific ways of preparing food.

They like to either:

a) mash the hell out of something,
b) boil the shit out of something, or
c) deep-fry the life out of something!

WHAT AN ANGLOPHONE SAYS	WHAT AN ANGLOPHONE MEANS	WHAT A DUTCH PERSON UNDERSTANDS
How are you?	Hello	He wants to know exactly how I am feeling & I have to give an accurate & truthful answer
Correct me if I'm wrong	I know I'm right, but	She is unsure of what she is saying
That's not bad	That's quite good to very good	That's mediocre at best
Perhaps you would like to think about…	I would really suggest you think about this	A suggestion but I can do what I like
I was a bit disappointed that	I am quite upset with you	Not really important
Please think about that some more	Bad idea, I urge you to reconsider	They like the idea!
That's interesting	I might be mildly interested	They're impressed
You must come for dinner sometime	Just being polite (not an invitation)	I will receive an invitation very soon
That is an original point of view	You're just silly	They like my ideas!
I hear you	I agree with you	Not sure if she agrees or not
IMHO (=in my humble opinion)	I'm not really humble and you're wrong	He's unsure of his position

You reply truthfully & at length when a English speaker asks «How are you?».

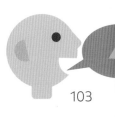

You think tipping means rounding the bill up to the nearest euro.

...and you pretend you need not follow the local tipping customs when abroad (*20% of the bill in America? They must be kidding!*).

You start sharpening your ice-skates at the first sign of freezing temperatures.

You may hear Dutch people grumbling about extreme cold weather, but secretly they love it and the excitement it brings to an otherwise dreary Dutch winter. Couple this excitement with the anticipation of . . . wait for it . . . skating on *natural* ice, and you have 16 million people on the brink of a national orgasm.

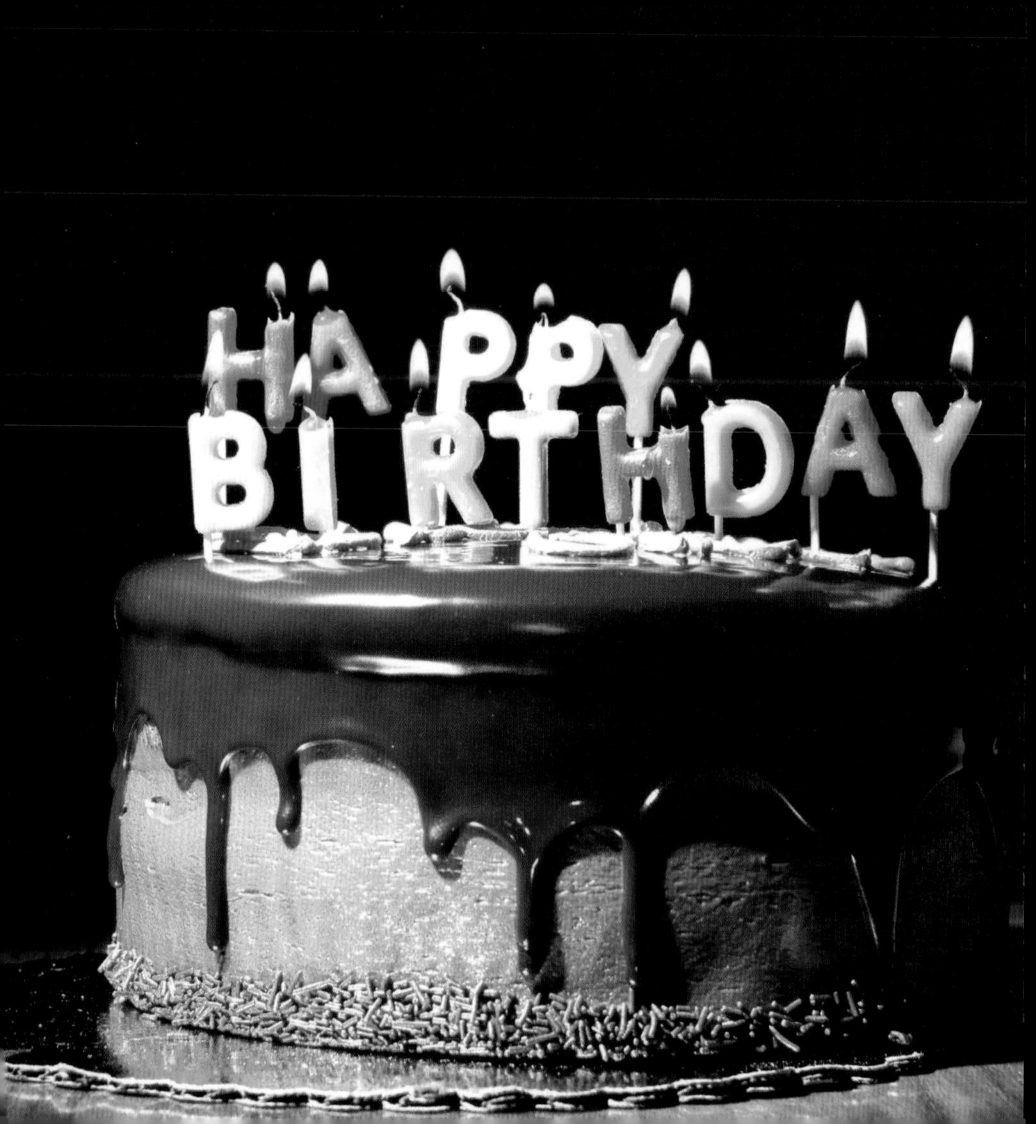
HAPPY
BIRTHDAY

You have to bring your own cake on your birthday.

Americans may have BYOB (bring your own booze), but the Dutch certainly take the cake (*pun-intended*) with their BYOC.

You're proud of the Sinterklaas tradition & tired of the Zwarte Piet debate.

The beautiful thing about culture is that it is forever fluid; adapting, and re-inventing itself over time. Luckily, progress has been made on the whole "black-face" front. One thing is for sure, the soot-smeared Piets look a whole lot less terrifying!! It's safe to say there'll be a few less toddlers having nightmares this festive season.

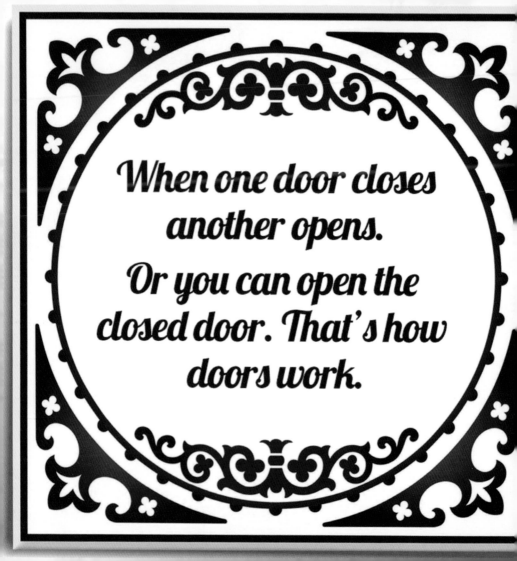

When one door closes another opens.

Or you can open the closed door. That's how doors work.

You have a Dutch wisdom tile somewhere in your house.

If you're a fan of Dutch directness and also enjoy some down-to-earth life advice, the Dutch 'wisdom tile' is for you! These so-called *tegelspreuken* have been doling out words of wisdom on pretty delft-blue tiles since the 16th century. After all, "*Van het concert des levens krijgt niemand een program.*"

It's raining pipe-stems

A monkey with a golden ring
is still an ugly thing

He who has butter on his head
should stay out of the sun

Alsof er een engeltje over je tong piest

You speak in expressions..., like a lot.

The Dutch spoken language is littered with literally thousands of expressions, metaphors, and idioms. Have a casual chat with any Dutchie and you are sure to find windmills, water, cats, and cows suddenly making their way into the conversation.

Need a cheat sheet for all that Double-Dutch? Luckily, we made one: our book Stuff Dutch People Say. #anothershamelessplug #canyoublameus? #doenormaal

You put mayonnaise on your fries (sometimes combined with satésaus and chopped onions!).

You don't know what lactose intolerance means.

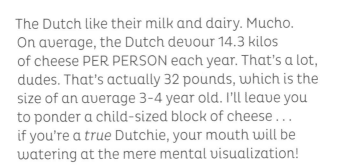

The Dutch like their milk and dairy. Mucho. On average, the Dutch devour 14.3 kilos of cheese PER PERSON each year. That's a lot, dudes. That's actually 32 pounds, which is the size of an average 3-4 year old. I'll leave you to ponder a child-sized block of cheese . . . if you're a *true* Dutchie, your mouth will be watering at the mere mental visualization!

in‚supera bility n.

nsupportable (‚insə'pɔ:...
tolerable; insufferable. **2** i
defensible.

▶ ‚insup'portableness n ▶

insurance (ɪn'ʃuərəns, -...
viding financial protecti
death, loss, or damage. **1b**
called: **insurance policy**. th
pecuniary amount of suc
turn for such protection.
insurance company. **2** a
risk or injury

You have insurance for everything.

In 2012, the Dutch National Consumer Bureau announced that far too many Dutch people were over-insured. Some even double, or triple insured. The spokesman was quoted as saying that purchasing insurance seemed to have become somewhat of a 'national hobby.'

YOU KNOW YOU'RE DUTCH WHEN...

You feel very generous when buying a 15 euro birthday gift for your best friend.

KEEP
CALM
AND
DOE
NORMAAL

You have told another person (or have been told yourself) to just «be normal».

I'm not going to lie. I might have told my four-year-old daughter this morning, as she screamed for more *hagelslag* to "*doe normaal!*". I'm pretty sure the sight of that scene would get me an automatic passing grade on the national *inburgerings* (integration) exam.

You know how to eat herring the right way.

No knives and forks for you: you're a real Dutchie and you know how to eat raw herring in one slippery, slimy, ooey-gooey bite! *Top!*

You love «salades» (aka suspicious sandwich spreads).

Most Dutch workers lunch on rather utilitarian sandwiches. However in recent years, the Dutch have upped their lunch game with the introduction of a multitude of mayonnaise-laden, gooey concoctions. Feeling adventurous? Why not try the *kipsatésalade* (blended chicken and peanut sauce), the *garnalenknoflooksalade* (blended shrimp, garlic, and mayo) or the *farmersalade* (blended mayo and farmer??).

129

You don't wear wooden shoes (but probably own a pair).

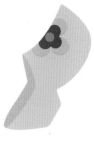

You have weird birthday traditions.

When Dutch people turn fifty, they are said to be either 'seeing Abraham' or 'seeing Sara.' Say what?! A biblical reference, although the original meaning is often debated. Celebrations typically included a cake or pastry in the likeness of the birthday boy or girl; however, over time the tradition has evolved to include a life-sized doll resembling the guest of honour! Think scarecrow-esque figures on front lawns, human paper-mâché giants, and five-meter-tall blow-up balloons of graying women (aka Sarah) or balding men (aka Abraham). Weird? Maybe a little . . .

You think umbrellas are useless.

You think being politically correct is something they do in other countries.

You've heard the rumours and I'm here to tell you they are, in fact, all true! Dutch people are direct. Direct to the point of #wtf. The Dutch speak their minds: there's no place for subtlety, nuance, political correctness, or tiptoeing around the topic. The Dutch get to the point — and take no prisoners!

You'd rather
do-it-yourself
than hire
someone.

You eat oliebollen on New Year's Eve.

Who wouldn't love deep-fried balls of dough covered in powdered sugar?! The smell of these calorie-bombs will have your mouth watering before you can even take the first bite. Nothing quite rings in the New Year like unabashed gluttony! #YOLO

You think King's Day is the best day of the year — except for when it falls on a weekend.

143

You don't mind Belgians, but it sure is fun to tell jokes about them.

Dutch people love to make jokes at the expense of their two favourite neighbours: the Belgians and the Germans! It's that good old 'big brother, little brother' complex found amongst many bordering nations, mixed with some lingering historic animosity and a healthy dose of sport-related rivalry.

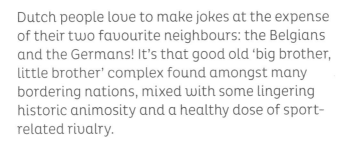

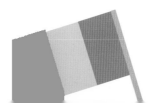

You make a hole in your stamppot for the gravy.

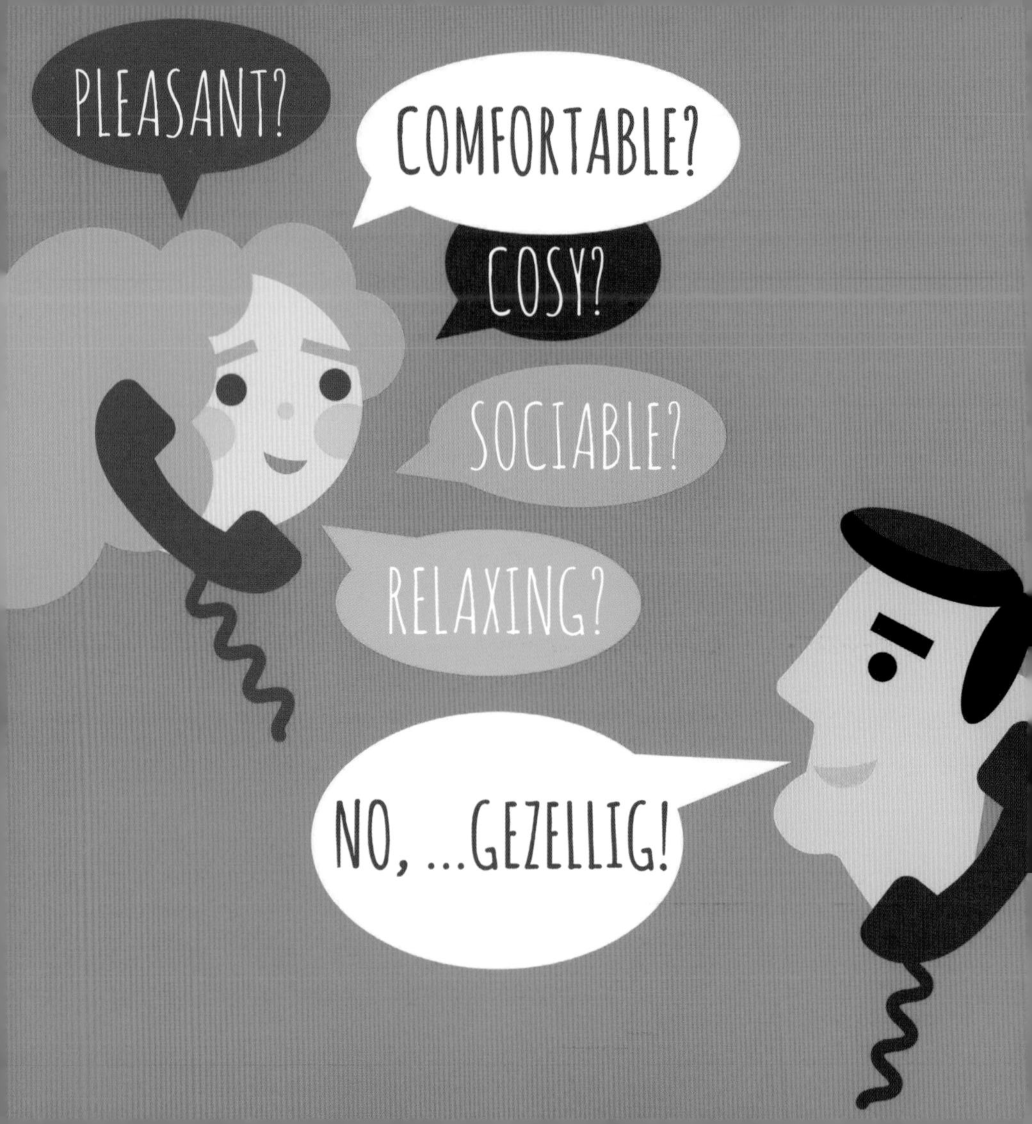
PLEASANT?
COMFORTABLE?
COSY?
SOCIABLE?
RELAXING?
NO, ...GEZELLIG!

You insist that any English translation for the word «gezellig» is never quite accurate.

You know what a «Hair salon» dish is (and you quite like it).

If french fries and shawarma had a baby, it would look a little like the infamous *kapsalon*. Take some fries, top with *döner* or *shawarma* meat, and add a layer of cheese (if you're really going to do it right: it should be Gouda). Melt the cheese and then top with lettuce/greens. *Eet smakelijk*!

You are a 183 cm (6 ft) man or 170 cm (5 ft 7 in) woman and consider your height to be just average.

Ever been inside a 16th-century canal house? Those small doors and quaintly low ceilings were indeed made for tinier people. In only a century's time, the Dutch went from being amongst the shortest nations to, in fact, the tallest humans on the planet.

You can
ride a bicycle
talking
on the phone
while carrying
your groceries
and 3 kids.

You don't care what others think of you.

This is how you drive your kids to school.

Who needs an ugly mini-van or gas-guzzling SUV when you've got a brilliant *bakfiets*. Load up the kids and pedal at your own pace!

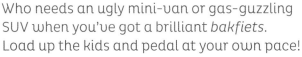

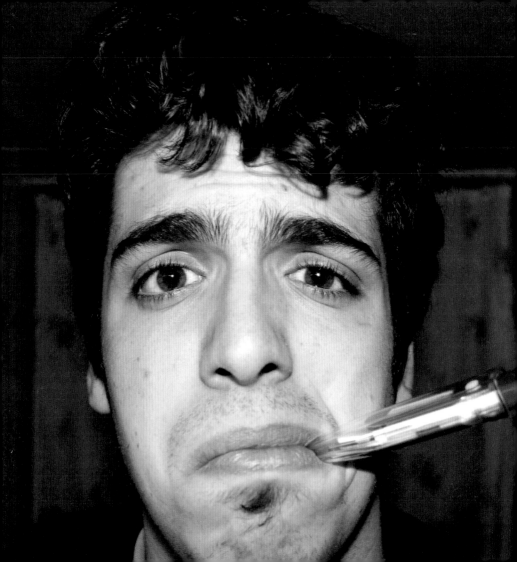

Your doctor will most likely recommend you take paracetamol for any ailment you might have.

Who needs a medical degree when they can simply advise (over the phone nonetheless) that any and all illnesses be treated by taking a little white magic round pill! *Hah! I shall open my 'Dutch-style" medical practice tomorrow!!*

All jokes aside, the doctors must be doing something right, as the Dutch healthcare system was just ranked the very best (!) in Europe for the seventh (!!) consecutive year by the Euro Health Consumer Index.

You invented the orange carrot.

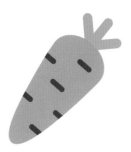

Carrots actually used to be yellow, white, and purple. But legend has it that in the 17th century, Dutch farmers cultivated orange carrots as a tribute to William of Orange who led the struggle for Dutch independence. #orangeisthenewpurple

You enjoy taking a look at the neighbour's apartment. They left the windows open!

You don't understand all the fuss about Gay marriage.

The Dutch are global leaders when it comes to tolerance and acceptance. Way back in 2001, the Netherlands became the first country in the world to legalize same-sex marriage. Since then, over 15,000 gay couples have married.

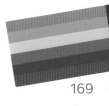

You speak German much better than you'll ever admit.

Kom op! Who do you think you're fooling!? According to the *EuroBarometer: Europeans and their languages:*

- 46% of the Dutch said they could "read news articles in German"
- 49% said they could "understand German broadcast news"
- ....and an immense 71% said they could speak German "well enough to have a conversation"! *Das kannst Du Deiner Oma erzählen!*

You think it's totally normal to take a "Daddy Day".

According to national statistics, over a third of Dutch men in the Netherlands work a reduced work week, many of them opting to take a day off work each week to be with their children. In a recent poll carried out by Statistics Netherlands, an astounding 66% of young men said they planned to reduce their working hours when they become a father! Woot!!!

173

You're a sun worshiper.

The Dutch are like sunflowers. Give them a little bit of sunshine and they will be found, en masse, out of doors with terrace chairs and heads pointed directly to the sun, bathing in the light. There is one thing that is certain in the Netherlands: if the sun is out, so are the Dutch.

You think marriage is just a piece of paper.

You know that old schoolyard rhyme: *"Sally and Ryan sitting in a tree. k-i-s-s-i-n-g. First comes love, then comes marriage, then comes Sally with a baby carriage."* Well, in the Lowlands, it seems the rhyme got reversed over time, as the Dutch get around to the whole marriage part well AFTER the love and the baby carriage(s).

This highly scientific formula here in the Lowlands appears to be: *attraction + love + buying a house together + having babies = marriage.*

177

You are simultaneously open minded and strongly opinionated.

You know that many English words such as cookies, brandy and booze come from Dutch.

Who invented English? The Dutch, of course!
Hundreds of English words come directly from
the Dutch language. Yankee, coleslaw, cruise,
skate, quack, landscape, spooky, buoy, skipper . . .
need we go on?

181

You don't necessarily like French people, yet still vacation in France every year.

You own a kaasschaaf.

. . . and know how to use it! The *kaasschaaf* (*'cheese shaver'*) was invented by Norwegian carpenter Thor Bjørklund in 1925. Mass production began in 1927, and shortly after it was introduced to the Netherlands. Most Dutch, Scandinavian, and German cheeses are suitable for slicing with the *kaasschaaf* due to their firm nature.

You don't really like guests dropping by unannounced.

You have funny birth traditions.

From the beloved *kraamzorg* to the *geboortekaartje*, *beschuit met muisjes* and the *kraamvisite*, the Dutch celebrate the arrival of a new babe with style and flare! The Dutch tradition of placing life-sized storks in windows or gardens is actually said to have 'flown' over from Germany.

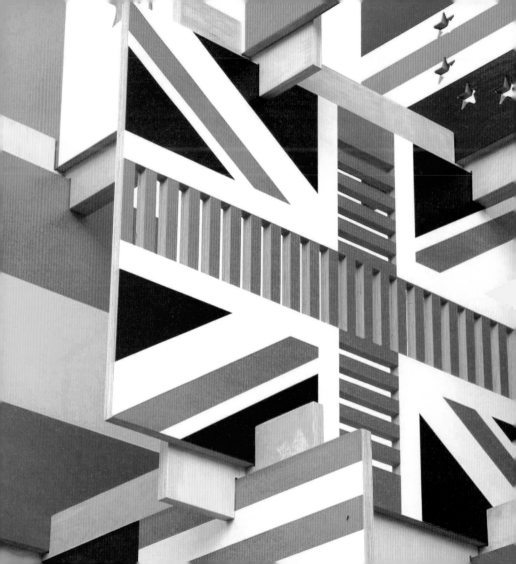

You speak three or more languages.

According to the European Commission's Eurobarometer, 77% of all Dutchies speak three languages or more. This is second only to Luxembourg, where 84% of the population can *parlez-vous* in 3+ tongues. Those Luxies (*is that a term?*) also claim that a mighty 61% of them can spreken in 4 or more languages; now that's just bragging!

You are
able to say
«achtentachtig
prachtige
nachten bij
achtentachtig
prachtige
grachten»
without getting
tongue tied.

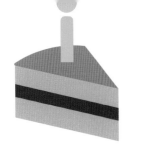

You've sat in many a circle at a birthday party.

195

You're a woman and don't really need your husband for anything.

You're a passionate collector of spaarzegels.

You know every word to at least two André Hazes songs.

- ☑ Bloed, Zweet en Tranen
- ☑ Zij Gelooft in Mij
- ☐ De Vlieger
- ☑ Kleine Jongen
- ☐ Geef me je Angst
- ☑ Een Beetje Verliefd
- ☑ Zeg maar niets meer
- ☐ Het is Koud Zonder Jou

You find yourself laughing aloud while reading this list.

About us

About the author

Colleen Geske is the blogger and best-selling author behind the hugely popular 'Stuff Dutch People Like' brand. Originally from Winnipeg, Canada, Colleen has called Amsterdam her home since 2004. Described as "blunt, provocative and wickedly funny", her blog and books offer an often satirical look at Dutch culture as seen through the eyes of an outsider.

About Stuff Dutch People Like

Stuff Dutch People Like is a celeration of all things Dutch. Started as a simple blog back in 2011, the Stuff Dutch People Like community now boasts a loyal following of over a half million fans in the Netherlands and around the world! The original Stuff Dutch People Like book was published in 2013 and became an instant international bestseller, with other books following suit! Visit us at www.stuffdutchpeoplelike.com

Our Books

"Blunt, provocative and wickedly funny", Stuff Dutch People Like is a satirical look at Dutch culture as seen through the eyes of an outsider. From Appelmoes to Zwarte Piet and everything in between, Stuff Dutch People Like covers it all—and then some!

From the creators of Stuff Dutch People Like comes this hilarious companion. Stuff Dutch People Say delves deep into the linguistic world of the Lowlands, exploring what happens when Dutch and English collide. From funny Dutch words, incomprehensible Dutch expressions and hysterical examples of Dunglish, we've got you covered!

Stuff Dutch People Eat is a comprehensive celebration of Dutch cuisine. Whether you're looking for festive sweets, traditional tastes or colonial classics, we've got something for every appetite! From breakfast straight through to dessert, Stuff Dutch People Eat will lead you through a culinary adventure spanning flavours—and centuries!

Stuff Dutch Moms Like investigates why Dutch moms are amongst the happiest in the world—and how they manage to have it all! Filled with hilarious anecdotes, tips and tricks, Stuff Dutch Moms Like takes an inside look at parenting in the Netherlands and the secrets to raising the happiest children in the world!